Discover and Share

BUGS

Angela Royston

W

FRANKLIN WATTS
LONDON • SYDNEY

About this book

The **Discover and Share** series enables young readers to read about familiar topics independently. The books are designed to build on children's existing knowledge while providing new information and vocabulary. By sharing this book, either with an adult or another child, young children can learn how to access information, build word recognition skills and develop reading confidence in an enjoyable way.

Reading tips

- Begin by finding out what children already know about the topic. Encourage them to talk about it and take the opportunity to introduce vocabulary specific to the topic.

- Each image is explained through two levels of text. Confident readers will be able to read the higher level text independently, while emerging readers can try reading the simpler sentences.

- Check for understanding of any unfamiliar words and concepts. Inexperienced readers might need you to read some or all of the text to them. Encourage children to retell the information in their own words.

- After you have explored the book together, try the quiz on page 22 to see what children can remember and to encourage further discussion.

Contents

Words in **bold** are in the glossary on page 23.

What is a bug?

Most bugs are insects.
All insects have six legs.

This bug is an insect called a ladybird.
You can tell it is an insect because it has six legs.

Every bug begins life inside a tiny egg.

Hungry bug

A caterpillar is a young insect.
When it is older, it will become
a butterfly.

A caterpillar eats
the leaf that it **hatched**
on. The caterpillar grows
bigger and bigger until
it is ready to turn into
a butterfly.

This caterpillar
eats and grows.
It will become
a butterfly.

I am a butterfly!

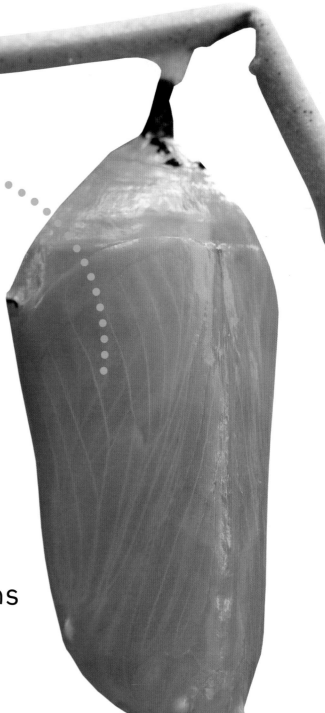

A caterpillar becomes a **pupa**. Inside the shell of the pupa, the caterpillar's body changes.

About two weeks later, the pupa cracks. A butterfly comes out and opens its wings. Then it flies away.

8

A caterpillar makes
a hard shell. Inside the
shell, it turns into a butterfly!

Flying bug

This bug can fly fast and slow. It can stop and stay still in the air.

This bug is a Hawker dragonfly. It has four wings and it is fantastic at flying.

It can fly backwards as well as forwards. It can even **hover** in the air.

11

Hidden hunter

This bug is a praying mantis.
It is hard to see because it
is the same colour as a leaf.

It hunts by sitting still.
When another bug comes
along, the praying mantis
grabs it with its strong front legs
and settles down for dinner!

**This bug is green like a leaf.
This helps it to hide.**

13

Busy bees

This bug is a honey bee. It uses its **antennae** to smell flowers and to taste and feel them.

The flowers make yellow dust called pollen. Bees collect the pollen and make it into honey, their food.

14

A bee flies from
flower to flower.
It is looking
for food.

15

Jumping bugs

This bug has long legs. It can jump a long way.

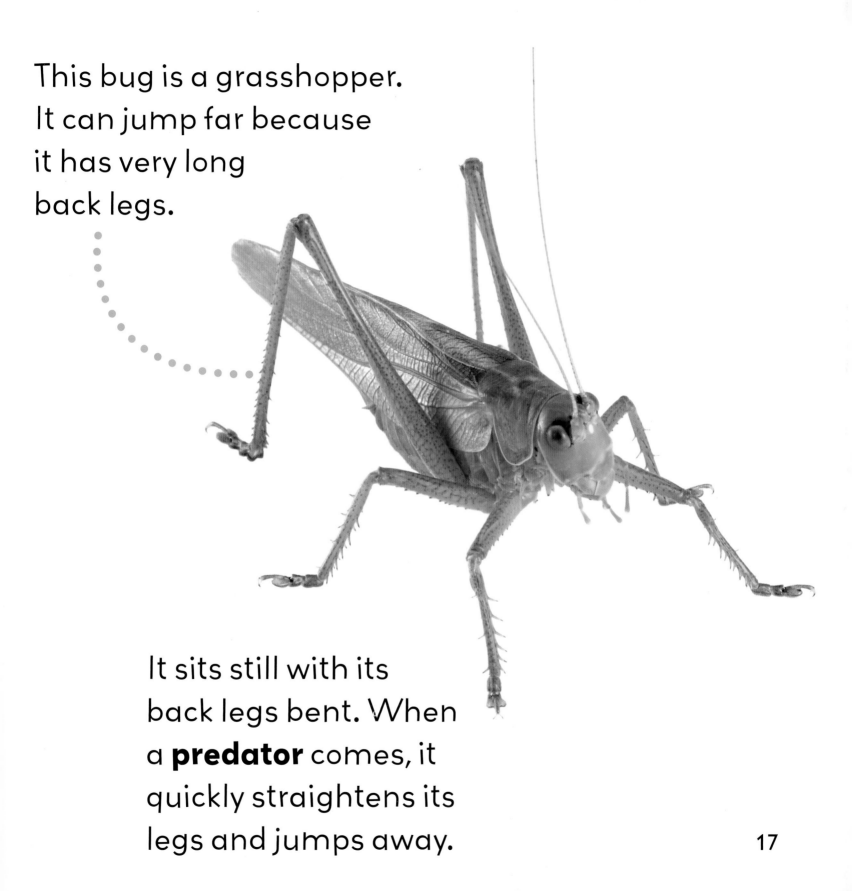

This bug is a grasshopper. It can jump far because it has very long back legs.

It sits still with its back legs bent. When a **predator** comes, it quickly straightens its legs and jumps away.

Bug home

These bugs are weaver ants. Many weaver ants live together in a **nest.**

Adult ants join the leaves together with **silk.** Young ants make the silk when adult ants squeeze them with their **jaws!**

18

These bugs
live in a
nest made of
leaves and silk.

19

Spinning bugs

This bug is not an insect. It is a spider. It has eight legs and no wings.

This spider makes a thin, golden thread. It uses the thread to spin its **web**. It traps small insects, such as flies, in its web and eats them.

This bug spins a web. It traps flies in the web and eats them.

Quiz

1. Which bug is eating this leaf?

2. How many legs does a spider have?

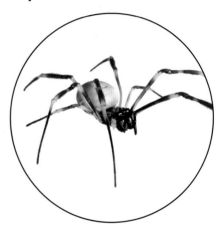

3. What happens when a grasshopper straightens its legs?

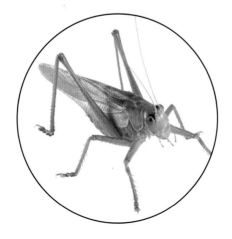

4. Which bugs made this nest?

22

Glossary

antennae the two long, thin feelers on the head of some bugs

hatch to break out from inside an egg

hover to stay in the same place in the air

jaws mouth and teeth

nest a place where bugs rest

predator a bug that kills and eats other bugs

pupa a caterpillar before it becomes a butterfly

silk a fine thread

web a fine net of threads

Answers to quiz:
1. A caterpillar.
2. Eight.
3. It jumps away.
4. Weaver ants.

23

Index

First published in 2013 by
Franklin Watts
338 Euston Road
London
NW1 3BH

Franklin Watts Australia
Level 17/207 Kent Street
Sydney
NSW 2000

Copyright © Franklin Watts 2013

ISBN 978 1 4451 1730 0

Dewey number: 592

A CIP catalogue record for this book is
available from the British Library.

Series Editor: Julia Bird
Series Advisor: Karina Law
Series Design: Basement68

Picture credits: alslutsky/Shutterstock: 4c. John Anderson/Shutterstock: 21.
Sue Bowden /Dreamstime: 3b, 11. Cameramannz/Shutterstock: 6. Chrom/
Shutterstock: 4br, 17, 22bl. Andy Heyward/Shutterstock: 7, 22tl. Stephen Inglis/
Shutterstock: front cover, 13. Eric Isselee/Shutterstock: 12. irin-k/Shutterstock: 5, 23.
kamnuan/Shutterstock: 4bl. Pavel Lebedinsky/istockphoto: 4tl. Andy M/
Shutterstock: 15. Bruce MacQueen/Shutterstock: 16. del. Monaco/Shutterstock: 3c,
9. Premaphotos/Alamy: 18, 19, 22b. Daniel Prudeck/Shutterstock: 3t, 14.
Peter Seager/istockphoto: 8. USBFCO/Shutterstock: 4tr. Peter Waters/
Shutterstock: 1, 20, 22tr. Konrad Wothe/Corbis: 10.

Printed in China

Franklin Watts is a division of
Hachette Children's Books,
an Hachette UK company.

www.hachette.co.uk

BETTWS

11 / 7 / 13